Creative Freelancing in the Gig Economy

Unleashing Your Creativity as a Freelancer

Matthew Macauley

DEDICATION

To all the passionate creators, the brave entrepreneurs, and the relentless dreamers who navigate the ever-changing landscape of the gig economy. Your commitment to your craft, your courage to chase your dreams, and your unwavering resilience inspire us all. May this book serve as a guiding light on your journey, empowering you to thrive and find success in the realm of creative freelancing. Remember, you hold the power to shape your own destiny. Keep creating, keep freelancing, and keep shining your unique light upon the world.

With boundless admiration,

[Matthew Macauley]

CONTENTS

ACKNOWLEDGMENTS

:

Writing a book is a collaborative effort that involves the support and contributions of many individuals. I would like to express my heartfelt gratitude to everyone who played a role in the creation of "Creative Freelancing in the Gig Economy."

First and foremost, I want to thank my family and friends for their unwavering support, encouragement, and belief in my abilities. Your love and encouragement have been instrumental in bringing this book to life.

I am deeply grateful to the team at the publishing house for their guidance, professionalism, and dedication throughout the entire publishing process. Your expertise and commitment to excellence have helped shape this book into its final form.

I extend my appreciation to the freelance community, fellow creative professionals, and industry experts who generously shared their experiences and insights. Your collective wisdom and expertise have enriched the content of this book and provided invaluable perspectives on the gig economy and creative freelancing.

I would also like to express my gratitude to the readers of this book. Your curiosity, passion, and pursuit of knowledge inspire me, and it is my hope that this book will provide you with the guidance and inspiration you seek as you navigate the world of creative freelancing.

Lastly, I want to acknowledge and thank all the freelancers who continue to shape and contribute to the gig economy. Your talent, creativity, and dedication are driving forces behind the ever-evolving freelance landscape.

To each and every person who has played a part in the creation and publication of this book, thank you from the bottom of my heart. Your support and contributions have made this journey possible and I am deeply grateful for your presence in my life.

Warmest regards,

[Matthew Macauley]

CHAPTER :1

Introduction

Welcome to "Creative Freelancing in the Gig Economy." In this book, we will explore the exciting world of creative freelancing and how it has become a prominent and rewarding career path in the gig economy. This chapter serves as an introduction, providing a comprehensive overview of the gig economy, its impact on traditional employment models, and the rise of creative freelancing as a viable option for professionals seeking independence, flexibility, and creative fulfillment.

1.1 Understanding the Gig Economy

The gig economy refers to a labor market characterized by temporary, flexible, and project-based work arrangements. It has gained significant traction in recent years due to various factors, such as technological advancements, changing work preferences, and the desire for a more balanced and fulfilling professional life.

Unlike traditional employment models, where individuals work for a single employer on a long-term basis, the gig economy offers a new paradigm where independent contractors, commonly known as freelancers, engage in short-term projects or "gigs" with different clients. This model provides individuals with greater control over their work, allowing them to choose projects that align with their skills, interests, and lifestyle preferences.

1.2 The Rise of Creative Freelancing

Within the gig economy, creative freelancing has emerged as a dynamic and thriving sector. Creative professionals, including graphic designers, writers, photographers, musicians, and artists, have found tremendous opportunities to showcase their talents, connect with a diverse range of clients, and shape their own careers.

The digital age has played a pivotal role in fostering the growth of creative

1

freelancing. With the proliferation of online platforms, marketplaces, and communication tools, creative professionals can now easily showcase their portfolios, reach a global audience, and collaborate remotely with clients from all corners of the world. This democratization of creative work has empowered individuals to leverage their skills and creativity, building successful freelance careers.

Creative freelancers also bring unique value to the gig economy. Their expertise and artistic abilities allow them to create compelling visual content, captivating narratives, and memorable experiences that businesses and individuals seek in an increasingly digital and visually-driven world. From designing logos and websites to crafting engaging marketing campaigns and producing captivating artworks, creative freelancers play a vital role in enhancing brand identities, storytelling, and overall customer experiences.

1.3 Overview of the Book

In this book, we will delve into the various aspects of creative freelancing in the gig economy, equipping you with the knowledge and skills to thrive in this exciting and rapidly evolving field. Each chapter will address key topics and provide practical insights and strategies to help you navigate the challenges and seize the opportunities that come with freelancing.

Here's a brief overview of the upcoming chapters:

Chapter 2: Navigating the Freelance Landscape
Chapter 3: Building Your Brand as a Creative Freelancer
Chapter 4: Finding and Landing Freelance Gigs
Chapter 5: Managing Finances and Pricing Your Work
Chapter 6: Delivering High-Quality Work and Client Management
Chapter 7: Expanding Your Freelance Business
Chapter 8: Balancing Work and Life as a Freelancer
Chapter 9: Legal and Ethical Considerations
Chapter 10: Future Trends and Adaptability in the Gig Economy

Throughout these chapters, we will explore essential skills, strategies, and best practices to help you establish a strong foundation, build a thriving freelance business, and navigate the evolving gig economy landscape successfully.

CHAPTER 2

Navigating the Freelance Landscape

2.1 Types of Creative Freelancing Gigs

The freelance landscape offers a wide array of creative opportunities for individuals looking to showcase their skills and work independently. Here are some common types of creative freelancing gigs:

Graphic Design: Freelance graphic designers create visual concepts for various mediums, including websites, logos, packaging, and advertisements.

Writing and Editing: Freelance writers and editors provide content creation services for blogs, articles, marketing materials, copywriting, and editing services.

Photography: Freelance photographers capture images for events, portraits, products, or stock photography, catering to diverse client needs.

Web Development: Freelance web developers specialize in building websites, creating web applications, and providing maintenance services.

Illustration: Freelance illustrators create visual representations for books, magazines, advertisements, and digital platforms.

Social Media Management: Freelancers in this field help businesses develop and implement social media strategies, create engaging content, and manage online communities.

Videography and Video Editing: Freelancers in this domain shoot and edit videos for various purposes, including commercials, documentaries, events, and social media content.

UX/UI Design: Freelance UX/UI designers focus on enhancing user experiences by designing user interfaces for websites, mobile applications, and other digital products.

2.2 Pros and Cons of Freelancing

Freelancing offers a unique set of advantages and challenges. Understanding the pros and cons can help you navigate the freelance landscape effectively. Here are some key points to consider

Pros:

Flexibility: Freelancing allows you to set your own schedule and choose your projects, giving you the flexibility to work when and where you prefer.

Independence: As a freelancer, you have the freedom to be your own boss, make decisions independently, and control your professional path.

Diverse Work: Freelancing offers the opportunity to work on a variety of projects with different clients, helping you gain diverse experience and expand your skill set.

Higher Earning Potential: Successful freelancers can often charge higher rates than traditional employment, especially as they build a strong reputation and attract more clients.

Location Independence: Freelancing can provide the flexibility to work from anywhere, allowing you to travel or relocate without being tied to a specific office.

Cons:

Irregular Income: Freelancers often face irregular cash flow, with some months being more profitable than others. It's important to plan and budget accordingly.

Self-Employment Responsibilities: As a freelancer, you are responsible for managing taxes, securing healthcare coverage, and handling other administrative tasks typically handled by an employer.

Client Acquisition: Finding and securing clients is an ongoing challenge in the freelance landscape, requiring consistent marketing efforts and networking.

Workload Management: Balancing multiple projects and deadlines can be demanding, requiring effective time management and organizational skills.

Isolation: Freelancing can be a solitary profession, lacking the social interactions and collaboration found in traditional office environments. Building a support network is crucial.

2.3 Building a Freelance Mindset

To succeed in the freelance landscape, it's important to cultivate a freelance mindset. Here are some key elements to consider:

Self-Discipline: Freelancers must be self-motivated and capable of managing their time effectively. Setting goals, creating schedules, and adhering to deadlines are essential.

Continuous Learning: Embrace a growth mindset and stay updated with industry trends and new technologies relevant to your field. Invest in improving your skills and expanding your knowledge.

Professionalism: Maintain a high level of professionalism in your interactions with clients and peers. Deliver quality work, communicate clearly, and uphold ethical standards.

Adaptability: Freelancers must be adaptable to changing client demands, industry shifts, and technological advancements. Embrace flexibility and be open to new opportunities.

Networking: Build relationships within your industry by attending events, joining online communities, and connecting with other freelancers and potential clients. Networking can lead to valuable collaborations and referrals.

Self-Care: Prioritize self-care to avoid burnout. Set boundaries, take breaks, and practice activities that recharge you mentally and physically.

2.4 Setting Realistic Expectations

Setting realistic expectations is crucial to thrive as a freelancer. Here are some key considerations when managing your expectations:

Finances: Understand that freelancing income can be variable. Create a financial plan that accounts for fluctuations and build an emergency fund for stability.

Workload: Be realistic about your capacity to handle projects and avoid overcommitting. Assess your time and energy limitations to set achievable goals.

Client Relationships: Building strong client relationships takes time. It's important to cultivate trust, communicate effectively, and manage expectations mutually.

Growth and Development: Recognize that professional growth as a freelancer takes time. Progress may be gradual, and success may come in increments. Be patient and persistent.

Learning Curve: Understand that freelancing involves acquiring business skills beyond your core expertise. It takes time to learn marketing, negotiation, and project management skills.

Competition: Freelancing can be highly competitive. Be prepared to differentiate yourself, develop a unique selling proposition, and continuously improve your skills.

By setting realistic expectations, you can navigate the freelance landscape with a clearer understanding of the challenges and opportunities that lie ahead.

CHAPTER .3

Building Your Brand as a Creative Freelancer

3.1 Defining Your Unique Value Proposition

As a creative freelancer, it's crucial to define your unique value proposition—the qualities and skills that set you apart from others in your field. Consider your strengths, experiences, and the specific niche you excel in. What makes your work different or more valuable compared to others? Identify the problems you solve for your clients and how your creative services bring unique solutions. This will form the foundation of your brand identity.

3.2 Crafting Your Personal Brand Identity

Crafting a strong personal brand identity helps you establish a consistent and recognizable image. Start by defining your brand's personality—think about the adjectives that reflect your style, tone, and approach. Consider how you want to be perceived by your target audience. Develop a brand voice that resonates with your clients and aligns with the work you do. Create a compelling brand story that communicates your values, passions, and mission as a creative freelancer.

3.3 Developing a Portfolio and Online Presence

Building a portfolio is essential to showcase your best work and demonstrate your skills to potential clients. Select your strongest and most relevant projects, and present them in a visually appealing and organized manner. Consider creating a website or using portfolio platforms to host your work. Optimize your portfolio for search engines by using relevant keywords and descriptions. Additionally, create an online presence on professional networks, such as LinkedIn, and join relevant industry communities to expand your visibility.

3.4 Leveraging Social Media for Self-Promotion

Social media platforms provide excellent opportunities for self-promotion as a creative freelancer. Choose platforms that align with your target audience and the type of work you do. Share your portfolio, client testimonials, and behind-the-scenes glimpses of your creative process. Engage with your followers by responding to comments and questions, and share valuable content that showcases your expertise. Collaborate with influencers or other professionals in your industry to expand your reach. Utilize social media advertising to target specific audiences and promote your services effectively.

Remember, building your brand as a creative freelancer is an ongoing process. Continuously refine and adapt your brand identity as you grow and evolve in your career. Stay consistent, be authentic, and consistently deliver high-quality work to establish a strong and reputable brand that attracts clients and sets you apart from the competition

CHAPTER .4

Finding and Landing Freelance Gigs

Finding and landing freelance gigs can be a challenging yet rewarding process for individuals seeking flexible work opportunities. The first step in this journey is to identify the right platforms and resources to connect with potential clients. Freelance marketplaces such as Upwork, Freelancer, and Fiverr offer a wide range of projects across various industries, allowing freelancers to showcase their skills and expertise. It's crucial to create a compelling profile that highlights one's experience, portfolio, and relevant qualifications to attract clients. Additionally, networking within professional communities, attending industry events, and leveraging social media platforms can help expand the freelancer's reach and visibility. Once potential gigs are identified, submitting well-crafted proposals tailored to the client's requirements is essential. Timely communication, demonstrating a thorough understanding of the project, and showcasing previous successful work can significantly increase the chances of securing freelance gigs. With persistence, dedication, and a strategic approach, freelancers can navigate the competitive landscape and find fulfilling freelance opportunities.

Once a freelance gig is secured, it's important to deliver high-quality work and maintain professionalism to build a strong reputation. Meeting project deadlines, being proactive in communication, and offering regular updates to clients can foster trust and long-term relationships. Freelancers should also be open to feedback and constructive criticism, as it provides valuable insights for personal and professional growth. As the gig progresses, freelancers can leverage their satisfied clients as references or testimonials to attract future clients. Additionally, actively seeking referrals from existing clients or asking for recommendations on professional platforms can help expand the freelancer's network. By consistently delivering excellent work, nurturing client relationships, and actively marketing one's services, freelancers can establish a successful career and enjoy a steady stream of freelance gigs.

4.1 Prospecting for Clients:

When it comes to finding and landing freelance gigs, prospecting for clients is a crucial step. Here are some tips to help you in this process:

Define your target market: Identify the specific industry, niche, or type of client you want to work with. This will help you focus your efforts and tailor your pitch accordingly.

Utilize online platforms: Explore freelancing websites, job boards, and online communities relevant to your field. These platforms can connect you with potential clients actively seeking freelancers.

Leverage social media: Establish a strong online presence by showcasing your work and expertise on platforms like LinkedIn, Twitter, or Instagram. Engage with relevant communities and share valuable content to attract potential clients.

Attend industry events: Attend conferences, seminars, and workshops related to your field. These events provide opportunities to network with industry professionals and potential clients who might require your services.

Ask for referrals: Reach out to your existing network, including friends, family, and former colleagues, and let them know about your freelancing services. They may refer you to potential clients or provide valuable leads.

Cold emailing and direct outreach: Research and compile a list of potential clients who align with your target market. Craft personalized and compelling emails or messages explaining how your services can benefit their business. Be concise, professional, and highlight relevant experience.

Offer free consultations or samples: Sometimes, offering a free consultation or providing a sample of your work can demonstrate your skills and value to potential clients. This can lead to future paid opportunities or recommendations.

Remember, prospecting for clients is an ongoing process. Continuously search for new leads, refine your approach, and adapt to the changing needs of your target market.

4.2 Networking and Building Connections:

Networking and building connections are essential for freelance success. Here's how you can effectively expand your professional network:

Attend industry events: Participate in conferences, meetups, and workshops related to your field. Engage in conversations, exchange contact information, and follow up with people you meet to establish lasting connections.

Join professional organizations: Become a member of industry-specific associations or groups where you can connect with like-minded professionals. Attend their events, participate in discussions, and contribute to the community.

Utilize online platforms: Leverage social media platforms, online forums, and specialized communities to connect with professionals in your industry. Engage in conversations, offer insights, and build relationships with potential clients and collaborators.

Offer value: Be proactive in helping others by sharing your knowledge and expertise. Offer advice, answer questions, and provide valuable resources whenever possible. Building a reputation as a helpful professional can lead to referrals and opportunities.

Maintain relationships: Once you've made connections, nurture and maintain them over time. Keep in touch with your network through periodic check-ins, sharing relevant content, or sending personalized messages on special occasions.

Seek mentorship: Identify experienced freelancers or professionals in your field who can mentor and guide you. Their insights and advice can prove invaluable in growing your freelance career.

Collaborate with others: Look for opportunities to collaborate with fellow freelancers or businesses in complementary fields. Partnering on projects can help you expand your network and gain exposure to new clients.

Remember, networking is a two-way street. Be genuine, supportive, and reciprocate the assistance you receive from your connections. Building strong relationships can lead to referrals, collaborations, and long-term success as a freelancer.

4.3 Pitching Your Services Effectively:

Crafting an effective pitch is crucial for showcasing your skills and winning freelance gigs. Consider the following tips when pitching your services:

Research your client: Before pitching, thoroughly research the potential client and understand their business, needs, and pain points. This knowledge will allow you to tailor your pitch to address their specific challenges.

Clearly define your value proposition: Highlight the unique value you bring to the client. Clearly articulate how your skills, expertise, and experience can help them achieve their goals or solve their problems.

Keep it concise and compelling: Keep your pitch concise and attention-grabbing. Focus on the most relevant information and use persuasive language to captivate the client's interest. Avoid jargon and communicate in a way that resonates with their needs.

Showcase your portfolio: Include samples of your work, case studies, or testimonials that demonstrate your capabilities and the positive impact you've had on previous clients. Visuals, such as an online portfolio or website, can enhance your pitch.

Customize each pitch: Tailor your pitch to each client, emphasizing how your services specifically align with their requirements. Avoid using generic templates or mass emails, as personalized pitches are more likely to stand out.

Be professional and confident: Present yourself professionally and exude confidence in your abilities. Demonstrate that you are reliable, responsive, and committed to delivering high-quality work.

Follow up: After sending your initial pitch, follow up with the client to ensure they received it and address any questions or concerns they may have. Following up demonstrates your dedication and may increase your chances of securing the gig.

Remember, effective pitching is an iterative process. Continuously refine and adapt your pitch based on client feedback and the results you achieve. A well-crafted pitch can significantly increase your chances of landing freelance gigs.

4.4 Negotiating Rates and Contracts:

Negotiating rates and contracts is a crucial aspect of freelancing. Here are some tips to help you navigate this process effectively:

Know your worth: Research industry standards and understand the value of your skills and expertise. Set a baseline rate that reflects your experience, the market demand, and the quality of work you deliver.

Determine your boundaries: Define your limits regarding rates, working hours, scope of work, and project requirements. Be clear about what you're willing to negotiate and what is non-negotiable.

Consider the project scope: Evaluate the complexity, time commitment, and potential long-term benefits of the project. Adjust your rates accordingly, but also ensure they are fair and sustainable for both parties.

Communicate your value: Clearly articulate the value you bring to the client and explain how your services will benefit their business. Focus on the positive outcomes they can expect from working with you.

Negotiate from a win-win perspective: Aim for a mutually beneficial agreement. Understand the client's needs and find creative solutions that meet their budget while ensuring your compensation is fair.

Seek a written contract: Always have a written contract that outlines the project details, deliverables, timelines, payment terms, and any other relevant clauses. This protects both parties and ensures clear expectations.

Be professional and respectful: Maintain a professional and respectful tone throughout the negotiation process. Listen actively, address concerns, and be open to finding common ground.

Consider long-term relationships: If the client is interested in an ongoing partnership, consider offering a discounted rate for a retainer or a bulk of work. Building long-term relationships can provide stability and recurring income.

Be prepared to walk away: If the terms or rates offered are significantly below your expectations or not feasible for your business, be prepared to decline the opportunity. Freelancing is about finding the right balance between fair compensation and satisfying client relationships.

Remember, negotiation is a skill that improves with practice. Reflect on your negotiation experiences, learn from each interaction, and continuously refine your approach to secure favorable rates and contracts.

CHAPTER .5

Managing Finances and Pricing Your Work

Managing finances and pricing your work are crucial aspects of running a successful business or freelancing venture. Effective financial management involves organizing and tracking your income, expenses, and investments to ensure a healthy cash flow. This includes creating a budget, setting financial goals, and regularly reviewing and adjusting your financial strategies. By carefully managing your finances, you can make informed decisions, anticipate potential financial challenges, and allocate resources effectively to optimize your business's growth and profitability.

Pricing your work appropriately is equally important as it directly impacts your revenue and profitability. Determining the right price requires considering various factors such as your costs, competition, market demand, and the value you provide to your customers. It's crucial to conduct thorough market research, analyze pricing models in your industry, and understand the perceived value of your products or services. Striking a balance between offering competitive pricing and ensuring a fair profit margin is key. Regularly evaluating and adjusting your pricing strategy based on market dynamics and customer feedback will help you maintain a sustainable business and maximize your earnings.

5.1 Accounting and Bookkeeping Basics

Managing finances is crucial for any freelancer or small business owner. Understanding accounting and bookkeeping basics is essential to keep track of your income, expenses, and overall financial health. Here are some key points to consider:

Separate Personal and Business Finances: Open a separate bank account for your freelance business to maintain a clear distinction between personal and business finances. This separation will simplify bookkeeping and help you track your business-related transactions accurately.

Maintain Organized Records: Keep detailed records of all financial transactions, including invoices, receipts, and expenses. Use accounting software or spreadsheets to track income and expenses systematically. This practice will make tax preparation and financial analysis much easier.

Familiarize Yourself with Accounting Terminology: Understand basic accounting concepts such as revenue, expenses, assets, liabilities, and equity. This knowledge will help you comprehend financial reports and make informed decisions regarding your business.

Track Income and Expenses: Regularly monitor your income and categorize your expenses. Income may include payments from clients, royalties, or any other sources. Expenses can range from office supplies and equipment to software subscriptions and marketing expenses. By keeping track of these, you can evaluate your profitability and identify areas where you can optimize your spending.

Reconcile Bank Statements: Reconciling your bank statements with your financial records is essential to ensure accuracy. Regularly compare your bank statements with your accounting records to identify any discrepancies and address them promptly.

5.2 Setting Your Freelance Rates

Determining your freelance rates can be challenging, but it's crucial to strike a balance between being competitive and adequately valuing your skills and expertise. Consider the following factors when setting your rates:

Calculate Your Costs: Begin by determining your total business expenses, including overhead costs, taxes, insurance, software subscriptions, and any other expenditures. These costs should be factored into your rates to ensure you cover your expenses and generate a profit.

Evaluate Market Rates: Research the market and determine the average rates for freelancers in your industry and location. This information will help you gauge the competitive landscape and adjust your rates accordingly.

Assess Your Value: Consider your experience, skills, and the value you provide to clients. If you have specialized expertise or a unique skill set, you may be able to charge a higher rate.

Consider Time and Effort: Assess the time and effort required to complete a project. Complex or time-consuming projects may warrant higher rates compared to simpler tasks.

Monitor Supply and Demand: Keep an eye on the demand for your services in the market. If you notice an increased demand or a scarcity of professionals in your field, you may be able to adjust your rates accordingly.

Be Flexible: As you gain experience and establish your reputation, you can gradually increase your rates. Be open to adjusting your rates periodically to reflect changes in your skills, market demand, or cost of living.

5.3 Estimating Project Costs and Pricing Strategies

When taking on new projects, accurately estimating project costs is essential for effective pricing. Here are some strategies to help you estimate project costs and develop competitive pricing:

Break Down the Project: Divide the project into smaller tasks and estimate the time and resources required for each. This breakdown will help you identify potential cost drivers and ensure you don't overlook any crucial components.

Consider Direct and Indirect Costs: Direct costs include expenses directly associated with the project, such as materials, subcontractors, and equipment rental. Indirect costs encompass overhead expenses, such as utilities, rent, and administrative costs. Consider both types of costs to determine the overall project cost.

Factor in Profit: In addition to covering your direct and indirect costs, include a profit margin in your pricing. This margin serves as a reward for your expertise and contributes to the sustainability and growth of your business.

Account for Risk: Assess any potential risks or uncertainties associated with the project. Consider including a contingency buffer in your pricing to mitigate unforeseen expenses or delays that may arise during project execution.

Competitive Analysis: Research your competitors and their pricing strategies. Analyze how your pricing compares to similar services in the market. This analysis can help you position yourself competitively and justify your pricing to clients.

Offer Options: Consider providing different pricing options to accommodate clients with varying budgets or needs. This approach allows you to cater to a broader range of clients and increase your chances of securing projects.

5.4 Invoicing, Payments, and Managing Cash Flow

Efficiently managing your invoicing, payments, and cash flow is vital for maintaining a healthy financial position. Here are some practices to consider:

Professional Invoices: Create professional and detailed invoices that clearly outline the services provided, the agreed-upon rates, and payment terms. Include your business information, such as your name or company name, contact details, and payment instructions.

Clear Payment Terms: Clearly communicate your payment terms to clients upfront. Specify the due date, acceptable payment methods, and any late payment penalties or discounts for early payment. This clarity helps avoid misunderstandings and ensures timely payments.

Track Invoices: Keep a record of all issued invoices and their status. Monitor which invoices have been paid, which are outstanding, and which are overdue. Consider using accounting software or online invoicing tools to streamline this process.

Prompt Follow-ups: If a client is late with payment, send friendly reminders at appropriate intervals. Maintain professional communication while firmly emphasizing the importance of timely payment.

Payment Options: Offer multiple payment options to clients, such as bank transfers, credit cards, or online payment platforms. This flexibility can improve convenience for clients and expedite the payment process.

Cash Flow Management: Maintain a cash flow forecast to project your expected income and expenses over a specific period. This forecast helps you identify potential cash flow gaps and take proactive measures, such as adjusting spending or pursuing additional projects, to ensure a healthy cash flow.

Reserve Emergency Funds: Set aside emergency funds to cover unexpected expenses or handle temporary income fluctuations. Having a financial safety net provides peace of mind and ensures your business remains resilient during challenging times.

By implementing these practices, you can establish a solid financial foundation for your freelance business, accurately price your work, and effectively manage your invoicing, payments, and cash flow. Regularly review and adapt your strategies as your business evolves to ensure continued financial success.

CHAPTER 6

Delivering High-Quality Work and Client Management

6.1 Understanding Client Expectations:

Understanding client expectations is crucial for delivering high-quality work. It involves actively listening to the client's needs, goals, and preferences, and clarifying any uncertainties to ensure a clear understanding. By gathering comprehensive information about the project requirements, desired outcomes, and timeline, you can align your work with the client's vision and provide a satisfactory end result.

6.2 Effective Communication and Collaboration:

Effective communication and collaboration are essential for successful client management. Regular and clear communication channels help build strong relationships, ensure alignment, and prevent misunderstandings. It is important to establish a communication plan that includes regular check-ins, progress updates, and a means for clients to provide feedback. Collaboration tools and platforms can facilitate smooth information exchange, document sharing, and real-time collaboration.

6.3 Time Management and Meeting Deadlines:

Time management is crucial in delivering high-quality work and managing client expectations. By carefully planning and prioritizing tasks, setting realistic deadlines, and efficiently allocating resources, you can ensure timely completion of projects. Regularly tracking progress, monitoring milestones, and adjusting plans as needed will help you stay on track. Proactive communication with clients regarding timelines and any potential delays is important for maintaining transparency and managing expectations.

6.4 Dealing with Difficult Clients and Conflict Resolution:

Dealing with difficult clients and conflict resolution is a challenge that may arise during client management. It is important to approach such situations with professionalism, empathy, and a focus on finding mutually beneficial solutions. Active listening, understanding the client's concerns, and addressing them promptly can help de-escalate conflicts. In some cases, involving a neutral third party, such as a mediator, may be necessary. Remember, maintaining a positive and respectful attitude throughout the process is essential for preserving client relationships and delivering high-quality work.

CHAPTER .7

Expanding Your Freelance Business

7.1 Scaling Up: Hiring Subcontractors or Employees

As your freelance business grows, you may find yourself facing a workload
that exceeds your capacity to handle alone. In such cases, scaling up by
hiring subcontractors or employees can be a smart move. Subcontractors
are independent professionals who work on a contract basis, while
employees are individuals you hire directly and provide with more
structured employment arrangements. Both options have their benefits and
considerations.

Hiring subcontractors allows you to delegate specific tasks or projects to
experienced professionals, reducing your workload and enabling you to
focus on higher-level responsibilities. It offers flexibility as you can bring in
subcontractors only when needed, without the long-term commitment of
employing someone full-time. However, managing subcontractors requires
effective communication, clear contracts, and quality control to ensure the
work meets your standards.

On the other hand, hiring employees provides more control and stability
over your business operations. Employees work exclusively for you,
allowing for closer collaboration and long-term commitment. You have the
opportunity to shape their skills and align them with your business goals.
However, hiring employees involves additional responsibilities like payroll,
benefits, and compliance with labor laws, which may require more
administrative effort and financial investment.

Deciding between subcontractors and employees depends on your specific needs, resources, and growth plans. It's essential to assess the nature of your projects, the required expertise, and your financial capabilities. Remember to clearly define expectations, establish strong communication channels, and consider legal and contractual implications when bringing others into your freelance business.

7.2 Diversifying Your Client Base

To expand your freelance business, diversifying your client base is crucial. Relying heavily on a few clients can put your business at risk if they reduce their workload or decide to seek services elsewhere. By diversifying, you can create a more stable and sustainable revenue stream.

Start by identifying potential target markets and industries that align with your skills and expertise. Explore different platforms, networking events, and online communities to connect with potential clients. Building relationships with a variety of clients across multiple sectors can help mitigate the risk of relying too heavily on a single source of income.

Additionally, offering a range of services within your niche can attract a broader client base. For example, if you are a graphic designer, consider expanding your services to include web design, branding, or illustration. This way, you can cater to the diverse needs of clients and increase your market appeal.

Maintaining excellent customer service and delivering high-quality work are vital when diversifying your client base. Satisfied clients are more likely to recommend your services to others, leading to new opportunities and referrals. Keep an open line of communication, listen to client feedback, and adapt your approach to meet their specific requirements.

7.3 Creating Passive Income Streams

Creating passive income streams can provide financial stability and boost your freelance business's growth potential. Passive income refers to money earned with little ongoing effort or active involvement once the initial setup is complete. While it may require upfront work, it can generate income even when you're not actively working on client projects.

One way to generate passive income is through creating and selling digital products. Depending on your skills and expertise, you could develop ebooks, online courses, templates, stock photos, or software tools that cater to your target audience's needs. These products can be sold through your website, online marketplaces, or platforms specializing in digital products.

Another option for passive income is affiliate marketing. Partner with companies or products relevant to your freelance niche and earn a commission for each sale made through your referral link. This can be achieved through blog posts, social media promotion, or dedicated email campaigns.

Investing in rental properties or other income-generating assets can also create passive income. While this avenue requires more significant initial capital and management, it can diversify your income sources beyond your freelance work.

Remember that creating passive income streams requires strategic planning, market research, and ongoing maintenance. It's important to choose income streams that align with your expertise and resonate with your target audience. Regularly evaluate and optimize these income streams to ensure they remain relevant and profitable.

7.4 Continual Learning and Professional Development

In the ever-evolving freelance landscape, continual learning and professional development are essential for expanding your business and staying competitive. Investing in your skills and knowledge enables you to offer more value to clients and opens up new opportunities for growth.

Stay updated with industry trends, best practices, and emerging technologies within your field. Attend webinars, workshops, conferences, and online courses that focus on relevant topics. Engage with professional communities and networks to exchange ideas, learn from others, and stay informed about the latest developments.

Seek certifications or accreditations that validate your expertise and enhance your credibility. This can be especially beneficial when targeting larger clients or competing for projects that require specific qualifications. Certifications can demonstrate your commitment to maintaining high professional standards and give clients confidence in your abilities.

Additionally, consider expanding your skill set by learning complementary skills or exploring adjacent industries. For instance, if you are a freelance writer, learning basic graphic design skills can add value to your services.

Diversifying your skill set can help you attract a broader range of clients and adapt to changing market demands.

Allocate dedicated time for self-improvement and professional development. Set goals, create a learning plan, and commit to continuous growth. Regularly assess your progress and evaluate the impact of your newfound knowledge on your freelance business. By investing in yourself, you'll increase your expertise, build a reputation as a knowledgeable professional, and position yourself for long-term success.

CHAPTER .8

Balancing Work and Life as a Freelancer

8.1 Setting Boundaries and Avoiding Burnout

As a freelancer, it can be challenging to strike a balance between work and personal life. However, setting boundaries is crucial to maintain your well-being and avoid burnout. Here are some tips to help you in this regard:

Firstly, establish clear work hours. Define specific times during the day when you will be available for work. Communicate these hours to your clients and stick to them as much as possible. This will help you maintain a structured schedule and prevent work from bleeding into your personal time.

Secondly, create a designated workspace. Having a separate area for work can help you mentally switch into work mode and improve your focus. It also allows you to physically step away from work when you're done for the day, helping you maintain a clear separation between work and personal life.

Thirdly, learn to say no. It can be tempting to take on every project that comes your way, especially as a freelancer. However, overcommitting yourself can lead to stress and burnout. Prioritize projects that align with your goals and values, and be comfortable declining opportunities that don't fit into your schedule or interests.

Additionally, take regular breaks throughout the day. Allow yourself time to recharge and relax. Engage in activities that help you unwind and rejuvenate. Whether it's going for a walk, reading a book, or practicing meditation, find what works for you and make it a regular part of your routine.

Lastly, remember to disconnect from work. Set aside dedicated time for your personal life, hobbies, and relationships. Engage in activities that bring you joy and help you maintain a healthy work-life balance. Avoid checking work emails or taking work-related calls during this time to fully immerse yourself in your personal life.

8.2 Time Management and Productivity Tips

Effective time management is essential for freelancers to optimize their productivity and maintain a healthy work-life balance. Here are some time management tips to help you make the most of your working hours:

Firstly, prioritize tasks and create a to-do list. Start each day by identifying the most important and urgent tasks. Break them down into smaller, manageable steps, and schedule dedicated time to complete them. By focusing on high-priority tasks, you can ensure that you make progress on essential work.

Secondly, utilize productivity tools and apps. There are numerous tools available to help freelancers manage their time and stay organized. Consider using project management software, time-tracking apps, and calendar tools to streamline your workflow and keep track of deadlines.

Thirdly, practice the Pomodoro Technique. This time management method involves working in focused bursts of intense work (usually 25 minutes) followed by short breaks (around 5 minutes). After completing four consecutive work intervals, take a more extended break (around 15-30 minutes). This technique can help you maintain focus and avoid burnout.

Furthermore, eliminate distractions. Identify the factors that often divert your attention and find ways to minimize them. Turn off notifications on your phone, close unnecessary browser tabs, and create a dedicated workspace free from distractions. By creating a focused environment, you can enhance your productivity and complete tasks more efficiently.

Lastly, learn to delegate and outsource. As a freelancer, you don't have to do everything yourself. Consider delegating tasks that are not within your expertise or that can be handled by others. This way, you can free up time for more critical projects or for personal activities that contribute to your overall well-being.

8.3 Self-Care and Well-being for Freelancers

Freelancing can be rewarding, but it also comes with its unique set of challenges. Taking care of your physical and mental well-being is crucial for long-term success and satisfaction. Here are some self-care tips specifically tailored for freelancers:

Firstly, establish a self-care routine. Incorporate activities that promote physical and mental well-being into your daily routine. This could include exercise, meditation, journaling, or engaging in hobbies that you enjoy. Find what works best for you and make self-care a priority.

Secondly, set aside time for relaxation and rest. Freelancers often have the flexibility to choose their working hours, but this can sometimes lead to overworking. Make sure to schedule regular breaks throughout the day and allocate time for proper rest and sleep. Taking time to recharge will improve your overall productivity and prevent burnout.

Thirdly, seek social connections. Freelancing can be isolating, as you may not have colleagues or coworkers around you. Make an effort to maintain social connections by joining freelancer communities, attending networking events, or scheduling regular catch-ups with friends and family. Engaging with others can provide support, inspiration, and a sense of belonging.

Additionally, practice mindfulness. Being fully present in the moment can help reduce stress and improve your overall well-being. Take breaks to focus on your breathing, practice mindfulness meditation, or engage in activities that bring you into the present moment, such as going for a walk in nature or enjoying a hobby.

Lastly, don't neglect your personal interests and hobbies. Freelancing gives you the freedom to pursue your passions, so take advantage of that. Set aside time for activities that bring you joy and fulfillment, whether it's painting, playing an instrument, or exploring new places. Nurturing your personal interests will contribute to your overall happiness and well-being.

8.4 Maintaining Work-Life Balance

Maintaining a healthy work-life balance is crucial for freelancers to avoid burnout and sustain long-term success. Here are some strategies to help you maintain work-life balance:

Firstly, establish clear boundaries between work and personal life. Define specific work hours and communicate them to your clients and colleagues. During your personal time, resist the urge to check work emails or engage in work-related activities. Create a physical and mental separation between work and personal life to ensure you have dedicated time for both.

Secondly, schedule personal activities and prioritize self-care. Treat your personal time with the same importance as your work commitments. Block off time in your calendar for activities that bring you joy, relaxation, and fulfillment. Whether it's spending time with loved ones, pursuing hobbies, or engaging in physical exercise, make these activities non-negotiable.

Thirdly, learn to delegate and outsource tasks when possible. As a freelancer, it can be tempting to take on every aspect of a project yourself. However, delegating certain tasks or outsourcing them to professionals can help alleviate your workload and allow you to focus on higher-value work or personal activities. Consider hiring virtual assistants or collaborating with other freelancers to lighten your load.

Furthermore, practice effective time management. Prioritize your tasks, set realistic deadlines, and avoid overcommitting yourself. Break down larger projects into smaller, manageable tasks and allocate dedicated time for each. By managing your time effectively, you can accomplish your work efficiently and create space for personal activities.

Lastly, don't neglect your physical and mental well-being. Take breaks throughout the day to rest and recharge. Engage in regular exercise, eat nutritious meals, and prioritize quality sleep. Additionally, make time for activities that reduce stress and promote relaxation, such as meditation, yoga, or engaging in hobbies you enjoy.

Remember, maintaining work-life balance is an ongoing process that requires conscious effort. Regularly evaluate and adjust your routines and priorities to ensure that both your work and personal life receive the attention they deserve.

CHAPTER .9

Legal and Ethical Considerations

9.1 Freelance Contracts and Legal Protection:

When engaging in freelance work, it is crucial to establish clear contracts that outline the rights, responsibilities, and expectations of both parties involved. Freelancers should ensure that their contracts cover important aspects such as scope of work, payment terms, deadlines, and termination clauses. Legal protection is vital to safeguard against potential disputes or non-payment. Seeking professional legal advice when drafting or reviewing contracts can provide freelancers with the necessary guidance to protect their interests and ensure a fair and equitable working relationship.

9.2 Intellectual Property Rights and Licensing:

Intellectual property rights are critical considerations for freelancers, especially those involved in creative fields. It is essential to understand and protect the intellectual property associated with your work. Freelancers should consider copyright, trademark, and patent laws, depending on the nature of their creations. Licensing agreements should be established to grant or restrict the use of intellectual property, ensuring that freelancers maintain control and receive appropriate compensation for their work.

9.3 Ethics and Professional Conduct:

Maintaining high ethical standards and professional conduct is essential for freelancers. Ethical considerations may include honesty, integrity, confidentiality, and respect for client privacy. Freelancers should be transparent about their capabilities, qualifications, and any potential conflicts of interest. They should also refrain from engaging in any unethical practices such as plagiarism or misrepresentation. Adhering to ethical guidelines not only builds trust with clients but also contributes to a positive professional reputation.

9.4 Taxation and Compliance:

Freelancers must be aware of their tax obligations and ensure compliance with relevant laws and regulations. Depending on the jurisdiction, freelancers may be classified as self-employed individuals, necessitating the payment of self-employment taxes. It is crucial to understand and fulfill tax requirements, including registering with tax authorities, maintaining accurate records, and filing tax returns on time. Compliance with other legal obligations, such as business licenses or permits, should also be prioritized to avoid penalties or legal issues.

By considering these legal and ethical aspects, freelancers can protect their rights, establish professional relationships, and maintain compliance with the applicable laws and regulations. Seeking expert advice when needed and staying informed about legal and ethical developments in their field can contribute to the long-term success and sustainability of freelance careers.

CHAPTER 10

Future Trends and Adaptability in the Gig Economy

The gig economy has been rapidly expanding in recent years, and its future trends indicate further growth and increased adaptability. One prominent trend is the rise of remote work and digital platforms, which enable individuals to engage in gig work from anywhere in the world. As technology continues to advance, the gig economy is likely to become even more accessible and flexible, allowing workers to choose when, where, and how they want to work. This adaptability is particularly appealing to younger generations who value autonomy and work-life balance.

Another future trend in the gig economy is the diversification of gig opportunities and skills. Traditional gig roles such as ride-sharing and food delivery will continue to exist, but we can expect to see a broader range of specialized gigs emerge. With the advancement of automation and artificial intelligence, certain tasks may be delegated to machines, creating new opportunities for human workers to focus on higher-level skills that require creativity, critical thinking, and emotional intelligence. As a result, individuals will need to adapt and continuously update their skill sets to remain competitive in the ever-evolving gig economy landscape.

Overall, the future of the gig economy looks promising, with increased adaptability and a wide array of gig opportunities. As technology continues to shape the way we work, individuals who embrace change and cultivate a diverse skill set will be well-positioned to thrive in this dynamic and fast-paced environment

10.1 Emerging Technologies and Their Impact

In the gig economy, emerging technologies are reshaping the way work is performed and creating new opportunities for gig workers. Trends like artificial intelligence (AI), automation, and blockchain are revolutionizing various industries and impacting the gig economy in several ways. Gig workers can expect to see increased utilization of AI-powered platforms that match them with suitable gigs based on their skills and preferences. Automation may streamline certain tasks, enabling gig workers to focus on more complex and creative aspects of their work. Additionally, blockchain technology can enhance trust and transparency in gig economy transactions, providing secure payment systems and reputation management for workers. As emerging technologies continue to evolve, gig workers must stay informed and adapt to leverage these advancements effectively.

10.2 Staying Ahead in a Changing Landscape:

The gig economy is characterized by its dynamic nature, with new platforms, industries, and trends constantly emerging. To stay ahead in this changing landscape, gig workers need to be proactive and agile. They should continuously monitor industry developments and trends to identify new opportunities and adjust their skills and offerings accordingly. Building a strong professional network can also be beneficial, as it can provide access to information, collaborations, and referrals. Additionally, gig workers should invest in personal branding, showcasing their expertise and unique value proposition to stand out in a competitive marketplace. Being adaptable and open to new experiences will allow gig workers to navigate the evolving gig economy successfully.

10.3 Embracing Continuous Learning and Flexibility:

In the gig economy, continuous learning and flexibility are crucial for long-term success. As technology advances and job requirements change, gig workers must commit to ongoing skill development. This may involve participating in online courses, attending workshops, or seeking mentorship to stay relevant and competitive. Adapting to new tools, software, and methodologies is essential for gig workers to offer high-quality services and maintain a competitive edge. Furthermore, flexibility is a key trait for gig workers, as they often face changing project scopes, deadlines, and client demands. Being adaptable and willing to adjust schedules and work arrangements will enable gig workers to meet client expectations and build strong relationships. Embracing continuous learning and flexibility allows gig workers to evolve alongside the gig economy and seize new opportunities as they arise.

CHAPTER .11

Conclusion

Throughout this book, I have embarked on a comprehensive journey, exploring the intricacies of creative freelancing and equipping you with the knowledge, skills, and strategies to thrive in the dynamic gig economy.

I began by understanding the gig economy and its impact on traditional employment models. I witnessed how the rise of the gig economy has provided fertile ground for creative professionals to showcase their talents, connect with diverse clients, and shape their own careers. I explored the various types of creative freelance gigs, enabling you to identify your strengths, interests, and areas of specialization.

Building on that foundation, I delved into essential aspects of creative freelancing, including building your brand, finding and landing gigs, managing finances, delivering high-quality work, and expanding your business. I provided practical insights and strategies to help you navigate challenges such as client management, negotiation, time management, and maintaining work-life balance. I also discussed legal and ethical considerations, ensuring you operate within the boundaries of professional conduct and protect your intellectual property.

As I navigated the evolving landscape of the gig economy, I explored future trends and the importance of adaptability and continuous learning. By embracing emerging technologies, staying ahead of industry developments, and embracing flexibility, you position yourself for long-term success as a creative freelancer.

But beyond the practical advice and strategies, I also emphasized the importance of cultivating a freelance mindset—a mindset characterized by self-motivation, discipline, adaptability, and a commitment to continual growth. I encouraged you to take ownership of your freelance journey, setting realistic expectations and forging your unique path to success.

Remember, freelancing in the gig economy is not just about work—it's about creating a fulfilling and balanced lifestyle that aligns with your passions and values. It's about leveraging your creativity and skills to make a meaningful impact on the world. As a creative freelancer, you have the power to shape narratives, evoke emotions, and inspire change through your work.

As you embark on your freelance journey, continue to foster a spirit of curiosity, embrace challenges as opportunities for growth, and cultivate strong relationships with clients and fellow freelancers. Collaboration, networking, and continuous learning will be your allies in navigating the ever-evolving landscape of the gig economy.

I hope this book has provided you with valuable insights, practical strategies, and inspiration to pursue your creative freelancing dreams. Remember that success may not happen overnight, but with dedication, perseverance, and a passion for your craft, you can thrive as a creative freelancer in the gig economy.

So go forth, embrace your creative freedom, and make your mark on the world as a skilled and empowered freelancer. The gig economy is your canvas, and your creative potential is limitless. Seize the opportunities, overcome the challenges, and enjoy the journey of creative freelancing in the gig economy.

Best wishes on your freelance endeavors!

About The Author

I am a seasoned professional who has deep experience and expertise in the field of creative freelancing and the gig economy. Drawing upon my years of practical knowledge, industry insights, and a passion for helping others succeed, I crafted this book as a comprehensive guide for aspiring and established creative freelancers.

With a background in the creative industry, I understands the unique challenges and opportunities that creative professionals face in the gig economy. I have witnessed firsthand the transformative power of freelancing and the immense potential it holds for individuals seeking autonomy, flexibility, and creative fulfillment.

Beyond my personal experiences, I have also conducted extensive research, staying abreast of the latest trends, technologies, and best practices in the gig economy and creative freelancing. I have immersed myself in the ever-evolving landscape, connecting with fellow freelancers, industry experts, and thought leaders to gain a holistic understanding of the freelance ecosystem.

My guiding principle has been to provide practical and actionable advice to readers. My writing style is engaging, informative, and relatable, ensuring that readers can easily grasp complex concepts and apply them to their own freelance journeys. My goal is to empower readers with the knowledge, skills, and mindset needed to thrive as creative freelancers in the gig economy.

With a genuine desire to see others succeed, I have poured my heart and soul into this book. I understand the challenges and aspirations of creative freelancers and are committed to helping readers overcome obstacles, unlock their full potential, and achieve their professional and personal goals.

My passion for creative freelancing and the gig economy shines through in every chapter of the book. By sharing my expertise, insights, and real-world examples, my aim to inspire and guide readers on their own unique paths to freelance success.

Overall, the my experience, expertise, and genuine dedication to the success of readers make them a trusted guide and mentor in the realm of creative freelancing. my commitment to empowering individuals to embrace the freelance lifestyle, pursue their passions, and create fulfilling careers in the gig economy make "Creative Freelancing in the Gig Economy" a valuable resource for aspiring and established freelancers alike.

9 798852 549914